Wild World

Watching Penguins in Antarctica

Louise and Richard Spilsbury

www.heinemann.co.uk/library
Visit our website to find out more information about Heinemann Library books.
To order:

  Phone 44 (0) 1865 888066

  Send a fax to 44 (0) 1865 314091

  Visit the Heinemann Bookshop at www.heinemann.co.uk/library to browse our catalogue and order online.

First published in Great Britain by Heinemann Library, Halley Court, Jordan Hill, Oxford OX2 8EJ, part of Harcourt Education. Heinemann is a registered trademark of Harcourt Education Ltd.

© Harcourt Education Ltd 2006
First published in paperback in 2007
The moral right of the proprietor has been asserted.

Editorial: Nancy Dickmann and Sarah Chappelow
Design: Ron Kamen and edesign
Illustrations: Martin Sanders
Picture Research: Maria Joannou and Christine Martin
Production: Camilla Crask
Originated by Modern Age
Printed and bound in Italy by Printer Trento srl

13 digit ISBN 978 0 431 19065 5 (HB)
10 digit ISBN 0 431 19065 8 (HB)
10 09 08 07 06
10 9 8 7 6 5 4 3 2 1

13 digit ISBN 978 0 431 19075 4 (PB)
10 digit ISBN 0 431 19075 5 (PB)
11 10 09 08 07
10 9 8 7 6 5 4 3 2 1

British Library Cataloguing in Publication Data
Spilsbury, Louise and Richard
Watching Penguins in Antarctica. – (Wild world)
598.4'717'09989
A full catalogue record for this book is available from the British Library.

Acknowledgements
The Publishers would like to thank the following for permission to reproduce the following photographs: Ardea pp. 18 (Graham Robertson), 19 (Graham Robertson), 23; Bruce Coleman p. 21; Corbis pp. 17 (Firefly Productions), 8 (Galen Rowell), 20 (Wolfgang Kaehler), 25 (Kevin Schafer), 27, 28 (Peter Johnson), 29 (Fritz Polking); Digital Vision p. 5; FLPA pp. 4 (Norbert Wu), 16 (Norbert Wu), 28 (Fritz Polking); Getty Images pp. 10 (PhotoDisc), 13, 22; Guillaume Dargaud pp. 7, 24, 26; NHPA pp. 12 (Kevin Schafer), 15 (Kevin Schafer); PhotoLibrary.com pp. 9, 14 (Daniel Cox); Science Photo Library p. 11 (Renee Lynn). Cover photograph of penguins reproduced with permission of Digital Vision.

The publishers would like to thank Michael Bright of the BBC Natural History Unit for his assistance in the preparation of this book.

Every effort has been made to contact copyright holders of any material reproduced in this book. Any omissions will be rectified in subsequent printings if notice is given to the publishers. The paper used to print this book comes from sustainable resources.

Contents

Words written in bold, **like this**, are explained in the glossary.

Meet the penguins

This is Antarctica, the home of many penguins. Penguins are black and white birds that live by and in the ocean. They cannot fly, but they can swim.

▼ *Penguins' black feathers stand out against the ice and snow.*

▲ The Adelie penguin is small and has a
white ring around each of its eyes.

There are eighteen types of penguin in the
world. We are going to watch emperor
penguins. They are the largest type.

Antarctica: a cold world

Antarctica is the coldest **continent** on Earth. Most kinds of penguins live in Antarctica. A few kinds live in warmer places.

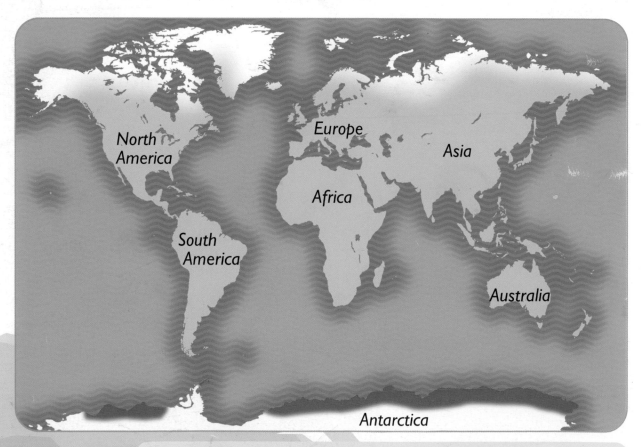

North America

Europe

Asia

Africa

South America

Australia

Antarctica

Key ● *This colour shows where penguins live in Antarctica.*

Freezing winds and snow storms blow across Antarctica. All year round the land is covered in ice and snow. There is little soil, so few plants grow here.

◀◀ *The Antarctic water is so cold that there is ice floating in it.*

There's a penguin!

Emperor penguins have a black head and back, with bright orange feathers in between. They are about as tall as a five-year-old child.

orange feathers

beak

▶▶ *The chubby emperor penguin has plenty of fat under its skin to keep it warm.*

wing

tail

Penguins have lots of small feathers that grow close together. This feathery coat helps to keep penguins warm in the cold winds. It is also waterproof.

▼ *This penguin is* **preening** *its feathers. It cleans them with its beak.*

Getting together

At the start of winter, adult emperor penguins meet up on the Antarctic ice. They meet to **mate** at special places called **rookeries**.

▶▶ *These penguins have come a long way from the ocean to their rookery.*

Now it is time for the **males** and **females** to form pairs. They call to each other. Males bow their heads to show off their orange neck to females.

▶▶ *Each female penguin chooses a male to mate with.*

Penguin eggs

A month after **mating**, the **female** lays one egg on the ice. In Antarctica there are no twigs to make nests. She gently rolls the egg to the **male** to keep warm.

▶▶ *The male balances the egg on his feet to keep it off the cold ice.*

*After laying their eggs, the females leave the **rookery** and go to the ocean to feed.*

It is the male's job to **incubate** the egg.
He keeps the egg warm until the female
returns. Emperor penguins are the only
birds that incubate their eggs during winter.

On the move

The **females** have a long trip back to the ocean. The penguins slide on their tummies on the ice when they are tired. This is called tobogganing.

▶▶ *Penguins push with their wings and feet when sliding.*

When they get to the ocean, the penguins can move more easily. They have a **streamlined** body shape. It helps them move fast through the water.

▼ *Penguins flap their stiff, flat wings up and down to swim along.*

Feeding time

The ocean around Antarctica is full of food for emperor penguins. The penguins dive deep to catch **prey**. They like to eat fish and squid.

▼ *Penguins can hold their breath for up to 22 minutes as they dive for food.*

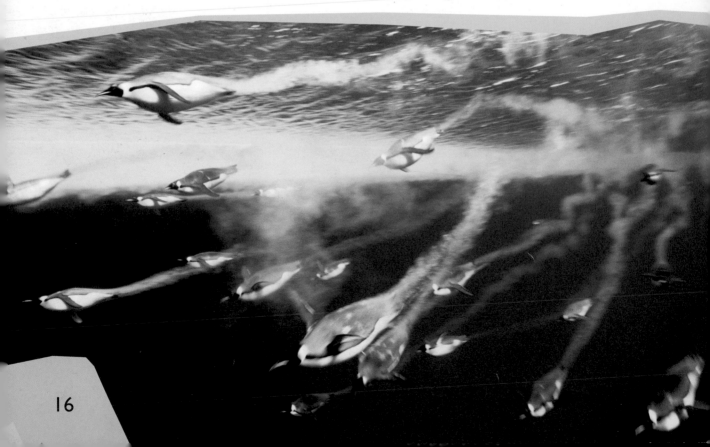

▲ Penguins can swim at least twice as fast as people can. They need to be fast to catch their prey.

Penguins have a curved, sharp beak. It grips their slippery prey to stop it escaping. Then the penguins swallow their food whole.

A long, cold wait

Winters are dark and cold in Antarctica. The **male** penguins **incubate** the eggs. A fold of skin covers their feet and keeps the eggs warm.

▼ *The males keep the eggs warm for two months while the chicks grow inside.*

The males shuffle close together and turn their backs to the cold wind. They take turns to stand in the middle of the group. It is warmest there.

▼ *Male emperors are the only penguins that huddle together in the middle of winter.*

Penguin chicks

The mother penguin returns after two months. She gets to the **rookery** just as the chick **hatches**. Now it is the **male's** turn to go to feed.

▼ *The emperor penguin chick is covered in thick, fluffy **down**.*

The fluffy chick stays close to its mother to stay warm. It cannot catch its own food. Its mother **regurgitates** fish from her stomach to feed it.

◀◀ *This penguin has returned from the ocean to feed its hungry chick.*

Growing up

The chicks get bigger and they need more food. They are old enough to be left alone. Both parents can go to fetch fish at the same time.

▼ *While most of their parents are at sea, chicks snuggle together to keep warm.*

One or two adults stay on the ice to look after the chicks. They are watching out for **predators**. Some big birds try to eat penguin chicks.

⏫ *Most emperor penguin chicks are so big that they are even safe from giant petrel birds.*

Ready to swim

This penguin is about three months old. Its soft fluffy **down** is dropping out. It is starting to grow proper waterproof feathers.

▶▶ *Penguins need all their adult feathers before they can go for their first swim.*

Leopard seals often catch young penguins that are learning to swim. Adult emperor penguins swim faster. They can usually escape from leopard seals.

▼ *This leopard seal is on the lookout for young penguins about to take their first swim.*

Summer days

December is the middle of the short
Antarctic summer. It is light all the time.
The penguins' land is still cold, but not as
cold as in winter.

▼ *In summer, some of the ice at the edge of
the* **continent** *starts to melt and break up.*

In summer there are lots of fish in the ocean around Antarctica. Young emperor penguins eat as much as they can. They need to grow fat before winter comes again.

▼ *If these young penguins get fat enough to survive the next two winters, they may have their own chicks.*

Tracker's guide

If you want to watch penguins in the wild, you need to find them first. You can look for clues they leave behind.

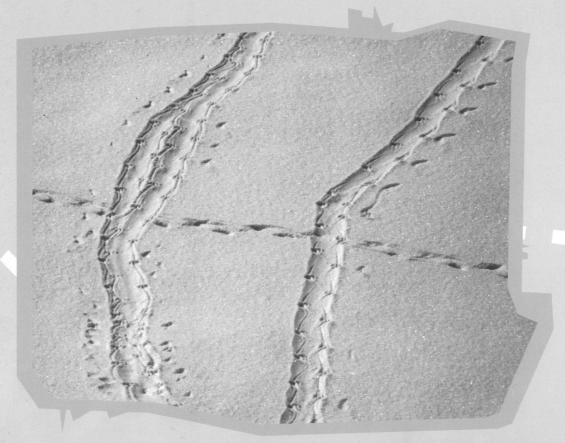

⬆ *You can find marks where the penguins have been sliding along on their tummies.*

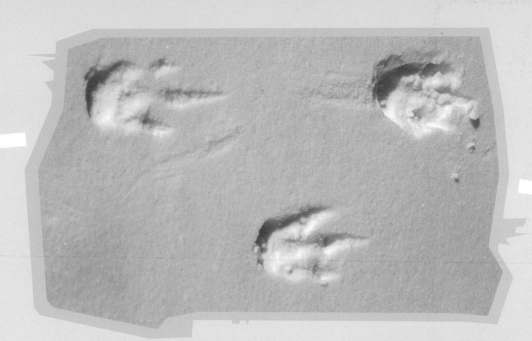

⬆ *In winter and spring, you can find penguin footprints in the snow.*

⏩ *Egg shells are often left behind when the chicks have **hatched**.*

Glossary

continent the world is split into seven large areas of land called continents. Each continent is divided into different countries.

down special, soft, fluffy feathers that keep chicks warm

female animal that can become a mother when it is grown up. Girls and women are female people.

hatch break out of an egg shell

incubate keep eggs warm so the chick inside can grow

male animal that can become a father when it is grown up. Boys and men are male people.

mate when male and female animals produce young

predator animal that catches and eats other animals for food

preening cleaning and oiling feathers

prey animal that gets caught and eaten by other animals

regurgitate bring up from the stomach

rookery place where penguins have their young

streamlined smooth shape to move through water easily

Find out more

Books

Antarctica: Land of the Penguins, Jonathan and Angela Scott
(Collins Educational, 2005)

Continents: Antarctica, M. Fox (Heinemann Library, 2002)

Life in a rookery: Penguins, Louise and Richard Spilsbury
(Heinemann Library, 2004)

Penguins, Patricia Kendell (Hodder Wayland, 2005)

Nature's Patterns: Animal Life Cycles, Anita Ganeri
(Heinemann Library, 2005)

Why am I a bird? Greg Pyers (Raintree, 2005)

Why do animals have wings, fins and flippers? Elizabeth Miles
(Heinemann Library, 2002)

Websites

Find out more about these amazing creatures at:
http://www.kidzone.ws/animals/penguins/facts.htm

Disclaimer

All the internet addresses (URLs) given in this book were valid at the time of going to press. However, due to the dynamic nature of the internet, some addresses may have changed, or sites may have ceased to exist since publication. While the author and publishers regret any inconvenience this may cause readers, no responsibility for such changes can be accepted by either the author(s) or the publishers.

Index